# Warren M. Washington

by Mari Bolte

T0027247

NORWOOD HOUSE PRESS

Cover: Warren M. Washington is an important climate scientist.

Norwood House Press
For information regarding Norwood House Press, please visit our website at:
www.norwoodhousepress.com or call 866-565-2900.

Hardcover ISBN: 978-1-68450-658-3
Paperback ISBN: 978-1-68404-999-8
eBook ISBN: 978-1-68404-279-1

**Library of Congress Cataloging-in-Publication Data**
Library of Congress Cataloging-in-Publication Data has been filed and is available at catalog.loc.gov

372N—012024
Manufactured in the United States of America in North Mankato, Minnesota.

# ★ Table of Contents ★

# Chapter 1

# Early Life

Warren M. Washington was born on August 28, 1936. He is from Portland, Oregon. He grew up with his parents and four brothers.

Portland sits below Mount Hood, part of the Cascade mountain range.

Washington joined the NAACP. The group supports Black people.

Washington always liked science. Anyone could do it. It did not matter if they were rich or poor. Skin color was not important.

Washington went to Oregon State University in 1954. He studied science and the weather. One year, he hiked up a mountain. He watched the weather from the top!

**Washington hiked to the top of Marys Peak in Oregon. Its highest point is 4,100 feet (1,250 meters)!**

# Chapter 2

# Sunny Days Ahead

Washington used computers. He made a model. It predicted future weather.

Washington's first models printed onto strips of film.

11

Over time, the weather changed. Washington studied the changes. Computers got more powerful. Now, Washington's models could do more.

**Washington worked for the National Center for Atmospheric Research for many years.**

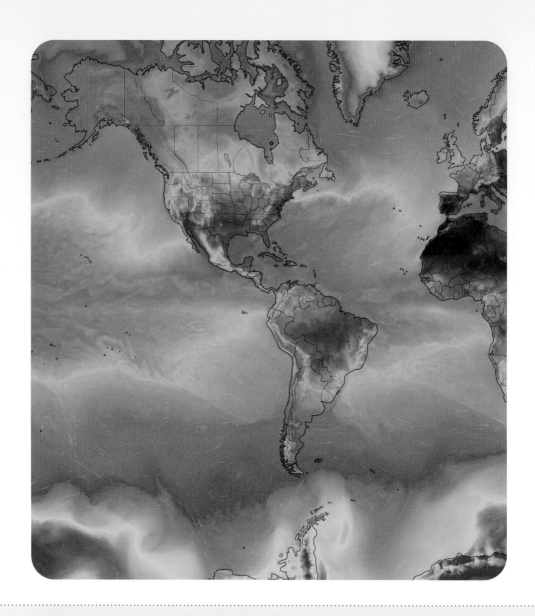

**Washington's models can create maps. Red is for places that are hot. Blue and purple mean cold.**

**Did You Know?**
Clouds and the night sky helped ancient people predict the weather.

Washington and his team made the models better. They added sea ice levels. Information on oceans was used. They also added $CO_2$ levels.

15

# Chapter 3

# Getting Warmer

People saw that Earth was getting warmer. They thought it was from the Sun. Washington used his models. The results said it was **climate change**.

> ★ **Large ships and planes create $CO_2$. This adds to climate change.**

**President Barack Obama awarded Washington the National Medal of Science in 2010.**

In 1975, President Jimmy Carter hired Washington. He would help the government study the weather. Washington worked with six different presidents.

Washington worked with many students. He encouraged Black people to study science. Washington **retired** in 2018. Today, the whole world still uses his models.

Washington sometimes works with his wife, Mary. She helped him write a book in 2006.

# ⋆ Career Connections ⋆

1   Meteorologists study Earth's atmosphere. They use information to predict the weather. With an adult's help, look up a meteorologist near you. Watch some of their forecasts. What types of tools do they use?

2   Computer scientists use all STEM subjects. They use science, technology, engineering, and math to create new computer tools. Imagine you are a computer scientist. What kind of computer tools would you create? Make a list with three different ideas.

3   Washington is a climate scientist. With an adult's help, go online to look up another climate scientist. What has that scientist taught us about weather on Earth?

4   Meteorology isn't just about weather on Earth. There are meteorologists who study space! With an adult's help, find out what the weather is like on another planet. Then, pretend you are on TV. How would you give a weather report on your chosen planet?

# ⋆ Glossary ⋆

**atmospheric** (at-muh-SFEER-uhk): Having to do with the atmosphere, the layers of air that surround Earth.

**climate change** (KLY-muht CHAYNJ): Shifts in weather patterns and temperatures over time.

**$CO_2$** (SEE-OH-TOO): Carbon dioxide, a heat-trapping gas that is created by the burning of fossil fuels.

**model** (MAA-duhl): A system where information on a certain subject is used to make guesses about the past, present, or future of the subject.

**NAACP** (EN DUB-uhl EY SEE PEE): The National Association for the Advancement of Colored People, a group started in 1909 to help Black people in the United States.

**predicted** (pruh-DIK-tuhd): Made a guess or statement about a future event.

**retired** (ruh-TYE-uhrd): Stopped working at a job.

# ⋆ For More Information ⋆

## Books

Parkin, Michelle. *George Washington Carver*. Chicago, IL: Norwood House Press, 2023. Read about inventor George Washington Carver.

Noll, Elizabeth. *Meteorologist*. Minneapolis, MN: Bellwether Media, 2023. Learn about STEM careers in meteorology.

## Websites

**Predict the Weather**
(https://kids.nationalgeographic.com/nature/article/predict-the-weather) Learn how to predict the weather by listening to nature.

**Warren M. Washington**
(https://kids.kiddle.co/Warren_M._Washington) Read about Warren Washington and his work.

23

# ★ Index ★

# ★ About the Author ★

Mari Bolte loves history and sharing its lessons with others. She has written and edited books on many different subjects. She lives in Minnesota surrounded by animals and the woods.